52 Ways to Reclaim Your Confidence, Feel Good in Your Own Skin and Live a Turned-On Life

DEBORAH KAGAN

Copyright © 2011 Deborah Kagan. All rights reserved.

No portion of this book may be reproduced mechanically, electronically, or by any other means, including photocopying, without written permission of the publisher. It is illegal to copy this book, post it to a website, or distribute it by any other means without permission from the publisher.

Deborah Kagan
8424A Santa Monica Blvd.
Suite 717
Los Angeles, CA 90069
323-650-4433
info@deborah-kagan.com
www.deborah-kagan.com

Limits of Liability and Disclaimer of Warranty

The author and publisher shall not be liable for your misuse of this material. This book is strictly for informational and educational purposes.

Warning – Disclaimer

The purpose of this book is to educate and entertain. The author and/or publisher do not guarantee that anyone following these techniques, suggestions, tips, ideas, or strategies will become successful. The author and/or publisher shall have neither liability nor responsibility to anyone with respect to any loss or damage caused, or alleged to be caused, directly or indirectly by the information contained in this book.

ISBN: 978-0-9840001-1-1

COVER AND INTERIOR DESIGN Ultimate Design VA www.ultimatedesignva.com

Praise from reader's of
FIND YOUR ME SPOT

"Deborah Kagan teaches, lives, models, and IS sensual. Wanna live your life on mojo overload? Read this and then live this."

~Suzanne Evans, www.suzanneevans.org

"I can't think of a better guide than Deborah Kagan. By using this book as your roadmap, she assists you in breaking free from the dead past to instead enjoy the glorious present moment."

~Steve Ross, Author of *Happy Yoga*

"If you could cross Mama Gena *(Mama Gena's School of Womanly Arts)* with Geneen Roth *(When You Eat at the Refrigerator, Pull Up a Chair)* you would get Deborah Kagan – a real world, straight talking, straight arrow heading right to the hearts of today's women, guiding us to fall in love with ourselves on every level."

~Lauren Solomon, Professional Image Expert

"Deborah Kagan has a deep understanding of how our immediate experiences shape our feelings and vision about ourselves . By taking a true look around us - a sensory inventory, if you will - we all have a chance to be more, see more, have more, and ultimately, love more. Any woman, whether entrepreneurial, or corporate, married or single, mother, sister or friend, will see herself differently after reading ME Spot. It all starts from page one."

~Amy Swift Crosby, founder, SMARTY
A Community for Networking Rebels
www.smartypeople.com

"No one is more qualified than Deborah Kagan to rev up your joy and turn the volume of your life up to 11. Try the easy and insanely enjoyable exercises in Find Your Me Spot. I absolutely positively guarantee....you won't be the same afterwards!"

~David Daniel Kennedy
Author of *Feng Shui for Dummies* and *The Feng Shui Home Study Course*

"Excuse me while
I kiss the sky."

- Jimi Hendrix

"I could not, at any age, be content to take my place by the fireside and simply look on. Life was meant to be lived. Curiosity must be kept alive. One must never, for whatever reason, turn his back on life."

-Eleanor Roosevelt

"The inconceivable
Becomes achievable
It's unbelievable
What you can do
Once that funny feeling
touches you."

- Bobby Darin

Contents

Acknowledgements		11
Foreplay		13

Section One — SEE ME

			17
#1	Lights, Camera, Action!		20
#2	Dreamweaver		22
#3	Show and Tell		24
#4	Steppin' Out		26
#5	Eye Candy		28
#6	A Picture's Worth A Thousand Turn-Ons		30
#7	Monkey See, Monkey's Mojo		32
#8	Mirror, Mirror On the Wall		34
#9	Let the Rhythm Move You		36
#10	Momma, Momma		38
#11	Moon Cycles		40

Section Two — TASTE ME

			43
#12	Firestarter		46
#13	Power Up		48
#14	How Sweet It Is		50
#15	Shake It Up		52
#16	Butter Me Up		54
#17	Chocolate: 'Nuff Said		56
#18	Get Messy		58
#19	Say "Ahhhhhh"		60
#20	Spice It Up!		62
#21	Breath of Life, Part I		64

Section Three — TOUCH ME

			67
#22	The Fabric of Your Life		70
#23	Royal Robes		72
#24	Animal Magnetism		74
#25	The Love Body Wash		76
#26	Touchy Feely		78
#27	Make Out with Nature, Part I		80

#28	Little Shop of Lovelies	82
#29	Flip Your Wig	84
#30	Plant Cosmic Seeds	86
#31	Truth Serum Letters	88

Section Four — HEAR ME — 91

#32	FUNK!	94
#33	The Call of the Wild	96
#34	Your Once Upon a Time	98
#35	Solo Sexy Time	100
#36	Mix It Up	102
#37	Curiosity Didn't Kill the Cat	104
#38	Noise Pollution	106
#39	Hear Ye, Hear Ye	108
#40	Body Talk	110
#41	Talk to Me, Baby	112
#42	Adult Story Time	114

Section Five — SMELL ME — 117

#43	Truth or BS?	120
#44	Playing with Fire	122
#46	Smoke Signals	124
#47	Bodacious Blooms	126
#48	Calgon, Take Me Away	128
#49	Common Scents	130
#50	Scents and Sensibilities	132
#51	Breath of Life, Part II	134
#52	Make Out with Nature, Part II	136
#45	Aromatherapy	138

Section Six — MORE, MORE, More — 143

#53	Your Date with Destiny	144
#54	Simon Says Stop	148
#55	Ride the Waves	150
#56	The Holy Trinity	152
#57	Girls' Club	156

Afterglow	*161*
About the Author	*167*

To all the women ready to take their life by storm, shine their light and be their most Sensually Empowered selves.

Here's to knockin' it all alive!

Acknowledgements

I stand on the shoulders of many people who have supported me to be where I am today. Some I've known for a long time, others not. Either way, they've all been influential in creating this book.

To Ofra Peters for consistently bringing me to the truth, year after year. To Michaela Boehm and the Sassy Seven, who never let me hide and always inspire me to be and give more. To Suzanne Evans for turning me from a HO to a BO. To Donna Kozik for creating a container and community to birth this book. To Wendy Hammers and DJ Eldon for reminding me I am writer. To Steve Ross who reignited the Shakti and fans her flame. To the Kagans (Dad, Ali, Jo, Eve, Elaine and Jeremy) for being *la familgia* and my ever-staunch cheerleaders. To my Mom for giving me one of the greatest sensual gifts ever—the opportunity to live in Italy at sixteen years old. That was the beginning of finding my ME spot! To my lady tribe: Amy, Angela, Audrey, Liz, Lisa, Heather, Jane, Jules, Kay, Rie and Wanda, for being bodaciously alive and sharing all the flavors with me. To Lori Snyder for her editorial wizardry.

And to my love, Chick. You'll truly never know how insanely grateful I am for you and how my heart swells every time I see you. Thank you for unabashedly traipsing into my life and making it oh-so-much-more sensual.

Foreplay

"To be sensual, I think, is to respect and rejoice in the force of life, of life itself, and to be present in all that one does, from the effort of loving to the making of bread."
~James Arthur Baldwin

Think of this book as your new friend. The friend that's always ready to play. The one that's up for an adventure. The one that lovingly kicks your ass when all you're thinking about is curling up in a ball and hiding under the covers. I wrote this book for you to have an all-season, all-wear, always-stylish, open-24/7 cohort in your quest to live a juicy, turned-on life.

The book is based on your senses because living a turned-on life means that you are sensually alive. The kind of alive where every cell in your body is plump, bursting with feeling and oozing excitement. This happens when you relish in your gift of sensuality, as only women can do.

> **sen•su•al** *adj* \'sen(t)-sh(ə-)wəl, -shəl\
>
> 1: relating to or consisting in the gratification of the senses or the indulgence of appetite: fleshly
>
> 2: sensory 1
>
> 3*a*: devoted to or preoccupied with the senses or appetites
>
>   *b*: voluptuous
>
>   — sen•su•al•i•ty *noun*
>   — sen•su•al•ly *adverb*

Your sensual nature is often confused as being sexual. While the two can overlap, they are not one and the same. Your sexuality is directly related to intercourse and all the physical bits leading up to it. We'll leave that for a future book (or two!). Sensuality is an innate gift of being human. It intensifies things—in both positive ways and not.

In order to truly harness your most confident self, you must crack wide open. You've got to put on a miner's hat with the goofy headlamp and crawl right up in there. Check out each and every nuance of your glorious self. Let this book be your guide.

I know we're all über-busy these days—there are kids to carpool, paperwork to file, bills to pay, errands to run, projects to tackle, relationships to be had, relationships to be nurtured, relationships to be dumped, movies to see, clothes to buy and meals to be made. I know. I know. I've been there. I'm just like you.

Here's the thing. All that stuff isn't going away.

And neither are you. So why not find out what you're really made of and let HER rip?!

There are over fifty-two ways in this book for you to explore your ME spot. That's one a week, plus a few extra in case you feel like really getting jiggy with it. You can read from cover to cover, working your way through one lesson at a time, or let your spirit lead you—randomly open to a new page each week. Either way, when you follow and integrate this information for one year <u>you will</u> see the REAL you emerge. Guaranteed.

No one can do this for you.

I've extended my hand as your guide and I'll hoot and holler for you along the way (trust me on this one…or ask my neighbors who think I'm cool, albeit pretty eccentric, every time I turn on the cosmic cheerleading portion of my day). But this is about you discovering your special place, *your* ME spot! I hear her calling your name. Go on and meet her.

Sensually Yours,

Santa Monica, CA
September 4, 2011

Section One

SEE
ME

Sense-sational Facts

Most people blink every 2-10 seconds.

Each time you blink, you shut your eyes for 0.3 seconds, which means your eyes are closed at least 30 minutes a day just from blinking.

If you only had one eye, everything would appear two-dimensional. (This does not work just by closing one eye.)

Owls can see a mouse moving over 150 feet away with light no brighter than a candle.

The reason cats' and dogs' eyes glow at night is because of silver mirrors in the back of their eyes called the tapetum. This makes it easier for them to see at night.

An ostrich has eyes that are two inches across. Each eye weighs more than its brain.

A chameleon's eyes can look in opposite directions at the same time.

A newborn baby sees the world upside down because it takes some time for the baby's brain to learn to turn the picture right-side up.

One in every twelve males is color blind.

# See ME

Your eyes are the video cameras of your life. They record every piece of data from the moment you wake up to the moment you go to sleep. Every day. Everything you look at is sent to your "hard drive"—aka your brain—for final processing. Your sense of sight is a complex and brilliant way you connect with life.

What you put in your scope of vision each and every day will not only shape how you feel about your life in the present, it will inform where you are going in your future. Surround yourself with things, people and places that stimulate and inspire you. If these aren't part of your life at this very moment, find concrete images of these things that you can use. I've gone to the point of driving a completely different route home in order to look at specific things/places that invoke what I'm CHOOSING to create in my life.

#1

Lights, Camera, Action!

Movies are a great way to step out of your day-to-day and live vicariously through characters on a screen. More than mere escapism, movies can guide you to deeper parts of yourself. They can prod you to ask questions you might normally ignore. And they can change the way you view certain places, people, clothing, and even everyday kitchen supplies (think Marlon Brando and the butter in *Last Tango in Paris*).

- Choose movies that inspire you.
- Choose movies that are sexy to you.
- Choose movies that involve people doing things you'd like to do.

By watching these movies, you'll visually take in information to ignite your inner spark.

Here are a few of my favorites to get you started:

Henry and June
Dangerous Beauty
Secretary
Bliss
Betty Blue
Last Tango in Paris
9½ Weeks

DEBORAH KAGAN

SEE ME notes

~ANAIS NIN

"And the day came when the risk to remain tight in a bud was more painful than the risk it took to blossom."

#2

Dreamweaver

Get in touch with the WHO, WHAT and WHERE that makes your blood pump just that much more powerfully through your veins. *There is something that excites you. There is someone who makes your eyes twinkle. There is a place that fills your body with breath.* Don't think about it. Feel into it. SEE it in your mind's eye. Is it a piece of art? A singer? An actor? A stranger you saw at the gym? The beach? The mountains? The city? These are the things that flush your cheeks and make you feel ALIVE. When you have these pictures in your mind, it brings you into a higher state of consciousness with a lot more energy.

ACTION

Vision Boarding is a popular tool to bring these images to life. Get a stack of magazines, catalogues, art books, postcards, greeting cards and any other inspirational materials. Other supplies you'll want to have on hand are stickers, glitter, colored pens, glue, tape, scissors and pushpins. Set a timer (I suggest no more than an hour) to sift through all your visual materials. Pick out the ones that draw you in. It doesn't matter if it makes sense or not. Cut out the ones that light up your eyes. Once you have your stack of images, take a poster board or large corkboard and arrange the images on it. Then add further decoration with the pens, glitter or other art supplies. When you're done, you have a VISION BOARD.

Make sure to put it where you can see it daily. It will remind you of what turns you on and what you're choosing to create in your life.

SEE ME notes

~MARGARET DELAND
"One must desire something to be alive."

FIND YOUR ME SPOT

Show and Tell

One of my all time favorite concerts was Prince. I believe he's the best performer the modern-day world has ever seen. He knows about *working the groove*. For a man in his early fifties, Prince is an incredible example of what's possible. The way he moves, dances, jumps and struts across the stage for HOURS is nothing short of knowing how to tap into vital energy. Prince pays attention to all the details. His wardrobe is precise and artful, from the shoes to the jewels. The colors on stage (lighting, other artists' clothing, confetti, set dressing, etc.) are nothing short of yummy eye candy. He knows that all these little things make a BIG difference in the overall experience.

ACTION

Attend a concert or media event (live or watch one on TV). Pay attention to the costumes, the lights, the dancing and the audience. Watch the visual feast unfold in front of you. Notice how it makes you feel. Are you inspired? What can you tweak in your life (personally or professionally) that would bring more meaning through a small detail?

DEBORAH KAGAN

SEE ME notes

~GOETHE
"Knowing is not enough; we must act.
Willing is not enough; we must do.."

#4

> "Twenty years from now you will be more disappointed
> by the things you didn't do than by the ones you did do.
> So throw off the bowlines, sail away from the safe harbor.
> Catch the trade winds in your sails. Explore. Dream. Discover."
>
> ~ MARK TWAIN

Mark Twain's said a lot of profound things in his time and this is one of the best. Travel allows you to bear witness to new people, places and things. You are privy to a whole host of stimuli outside of your norm. It's something EVERYONE can do.

You don't have to book a trip to Fiji (although that sounds really good, doesn't it?!). You can simply go to another part of the town where you live. What ethnic neighborhoods are near you? Is there a town or village within driving distance? How about taking a bus or train trip an hour away? Get out in the world and see what it has to offer. Exploring other areas, cultures and geographic destinations sparks ideas. Ideas spark inner flame. Inner flame means turned on!

SEE ME notes

~MIRIAM BEARD

"Certainly, travel is more than the seeing of sights; it is a change that goes on, deep and permanent, in the ideas of living."

#5

Eye Candy

It's common to hear that men are visual creatures. However, when it comes to window-shopping, women take the cake. The beauty of strolling down the street, stopping every few moments to drink in a silk dress, a modern couch, a pair of devilish shoes or a blingy ring in a window is femmeporn. It's common knowledge that women's magazines have been used for the same thing. However, these magazines are actually detrimental to your turn-on because they distort body image and much more.

Window-shopping is a healthy version of style stimuli. Not only do you get to explore the things you like, you're moving your body at the same time. Double endorphin whammy!

ACTION

Take yourself on a window-shopping date.

SEE *ME* notes

~SOPHOCLES

"One learns by doing the thing; for though you think you know it, you have no certainty until you try."

A Picture's Worth a Thousand Turn-Ons

For thousands of years, art has inspired millions. Paintings, sculptures, photography and multimedia are all various forms that prod, nudge and seduce us. The artists that created these pieces were all turned-on by something, and they took that inspiration to create art that would, hopefully, turn someone else on.

I remember the last time I spent a few hours in the Met museum in New York City. The building is steeped in mastery. It pours out of the walls. Of the few special exhibits on display at the time, I visited *American Woman* and *Picasso*. Both made my skin tingle. Both perked up my attention. Both brought a dose of fresh life into my system.

When you walk through museums or art galleries, you are forced to observe life at a slower rate. You are made to inhale images. This is a brilliant way to find what flips your inner switch.

ACTION

Visit a museum or art gallery. If you're allowed, take photos of the pieces that excite you, or purchase a postcard or poster if available. Bring these images home. You can frame them, put them on your refrigerator or pin them to the wall. Now you've got a constant visual to remind you of what brought you inspiration.

SEE ME notes

~STELLA ADLER
"Life beats down and crushes the soul
and art reminds you that you have one."

#7

Monkey See, Monkey's Mojo

Ladies, listen up. Your bedroom is at stake for holding your life captive. What I'm about to share is so important, it has the power to change your life right now. I suggest you take a deep breath with me (I'm taking one as I write this), and get ready for some serious goodness.

Your bedroom is exclusively for the 3Rs: Rest, Romance, Rejuvenation.

Anything that falls outside of that category is a distraction. If you're going to sleep and waking up every day looking at a work desk, you're contributing to your stress. If you're going to sleep and waking up every day looking at a whole bunch of electronics, you're contributing to the electronic noise in your life. If you're going to sleep and waking up every day looking at a whole bunch of laundry and clutter, you're contributing to mental confusion.

Your bedroom is the container for the closest thing to you—your bed.

We spend a third of our lives in bed! That could be up to thirty-plus years if you're like the women in my family. What this means for you is you must pay attention to what's going on *in, on* and *around* your bed.

Clear out any and all of the distraction (remember the 3Rs).

- Be aware of what's directly across from your bed. This is the thing(s) you see right before you go to sleep and immediately upon waking.
- Make your bedroom a visual haven.
- Let all the items, from the linens to the lamps to the little objects on your dresser, infuse you with positive, uplifting vibes.

DEBORAH KAGAN

SEE ME notes

~HAROLD B. LEE
"The most important work you and I will ever do will be within the walls of our homes."

#8

Mirror, Mirror on the Wall

Regardless if you're in a relationship or not, taking some ME time is the KEY to staying sane and healthy…even if you've got all your extended family visiting from Timbuktu and you're not going to see them again for ten years. You've got to give yourself at least FIVE MINUTES of what I call "Stop. Look. Listen."

Stop to actually look at yourself. For real. In the mirror. Look into your eyes. Breathe.

Look. Who's looking back at you? Not the skin-and-bones person. The other one, the one behind your eyes. Who's that? See that person. Check HER out.

Listen. She's the one with the truth. She's the one who knows you're sexy because you're so insatiably YOU. She's the one who wants you to put on the feather boa for the holiday party and line your eyes with the glitter. Go on and take a look. You'll be met with a love you might not have known was actually living IN you this whole time.

SEE ME notes

~EARL MAC RAUCH

"Remember, no matter where you go, there you are."

#9

Let the Rhythm Move You

Soaking in the sheer decadence of a burlesque show is an instant turn-on. Burlesque highlights all the beauty of women. It's curve-friendly. It's playful. And it's absolutely seductive.

There are usually artful, fantastic costumes to feast your eyes on…and oh, those shoes!

If you're shy to explore this type of outing, get a group of women together to share the experience. Then talk about what you saw. Hear what inspired the other women. Write down a few ideas of what you'd like to bring into your wardrobe or even take note of a few moves you'd like to try. You might find more of your own sassy rhythm and a new appreciation for your body.

SEE ME notes

~MARTHA GRAHAM
"Dance is the hidden language of the soul."

#10

Momma, Momma

Mother Nature was one smart cookie when she made all the things she did. The amount of visual stimuli in her back pocket is endless. Have you noticed the palette of colors that moves across the landscape of your day? How the morning light is so fresh, promising and raw? How the "magic hour" light at the end of the day makes lovers swoon? How the shades of green vary between the grass, leaves and bushes in your yard?

Nature offers a smorgasm of colors, layers, textures and more.

Take a look outside your window right now. What do you see? Is there something that amazes you? Is there something you've never noticed before? Or how about something that you see every day, but it's suddenly more meaningful to you?

- Choose to spend time looking deeply at nature.
- Allow it to permeate your cells.
- Let it invigorate your day.

You're guaranteed to be more alive inside when you marvel at what's right in front of you.

SEE ME notes

~FRANK LLOYD WRIGHT
"I believe in God, only I spell it Nature."

#11

Moon Cycles

I love the moon! "La Bella Luna" is what I affectionately call her—because the Moon is a SHE. Have you looked up at her lately? She's genuinely stunning. Brilliant, really. She moves in phases, and for hundreds of years people have observed her motion. The phases, generally referred to in quarters, represent different qualities and energies. She moves through the same phases every single month without fail.

The two important phases in which to watch her are the NEW MOON and the FULL MOON. The New Moon is when you receive a "pass go" card from the universe. What's so cool about this is that you have a chance to: **Stop. Breathe. Focus. Plant.** The Full Moon is when you receive illumined guidance. The groovy part about this is that you have the opportunity to **Stop. Breathe. Purge. Regroup.**

No matter what's happening in all our busy crazy lives, there's a constant cycle occurring with the phases of the moon. The moon's cycle is just one of the many cycles we are subject to on a regular basis (think the sun, the seasons, stages of life, etc.).

- Make sure to observe her.
- Moonbathe.
- Soak in her ancient wisdom.

As women, much of our body is affected by the moon's cycle (our menstrual cycle has been called "our moon."). Get friendly and share your secrets with her. She's been known to surprise many women with incredible blessings and their heart's desires.

DEBORAH KAGAN

SEE ME notes

~ISABEL YOSITO
"Stars that shine bling in the moon night, might
I find true love squirreled away tonight?"

Section Two

TASTE
ME

Sense-sational Facts

We have almost 10,000 taste buds inside our mouths, even on the roofs of our mouths.

Insects have the most highly developed sense of taste. They have taste organs on their feet, antennae and mouthparts.

Fish can taste with their fins and tail as well as their mouth.

In general, girls have more taste buds than boys.

Taste is the weakest of the five senses.

Taste ME

Your tongue and the roof of your mouth are covered with thousands of tiny taste buds. When you eat something, the saliva in your mouth helps break down your food. This causes the receptor cells located in your taste buds to send messages through sensory nerves to your brain. Your taste buds can recognize four basic kinds of tastes: sweet, salty, sour, and bitter.

What you put in your mouth each and every day will not only affect your overall health, it will dictate your level of excitement for life. There are the literal things we put in our mouths (food, beverage, medicine, supplements, body parts, etc.) and the figurative ones (words, thoughts, feelings). Ingest only those things that contribute to your highest self. Purge your surroundings of the people, places and things that leave a bitter taste in your mouth.

Your tastes will change as you grow and transform—which is part of the fun because you're guaranteed the opportunity to consistently shift things up and never be bored.

#12

Firestarter

It only makes sense to begin this section about TASTE with the kitchen. The kitchen houses one of the most important items of your home—the stove. The obvious conclusion about the stove is that is allows us to cook food and nourish ourselves with interesting things to taste. The not-so-obvious thing about the stove is that it is the energy generator of your life. It's like the engine in your car or the heart in your body. It takes the vital ingredient (in this case, chi) and moves it throughout your environment body. You can also think of the stove as your modern day fire pit. When you literally turn on the flames, more energy and enthusiasm is available to you.

ACTION

Ignite the burners on your stove, even if you don't cook. Make sure to use all of them. You don't have to use them all at once, but make sure to rotate in order to get an even distribution of "flavor" in your life.

DEBORAH KAGAN

TASTE ME notes

~CHARLES KINGSLEY
"We act as though comfort and luxury were the chief requirements of life, when all that we need to make us really happy is something to be enthusiastic about."

#13

Power Up

Living a turned-on life means that you have the energy and stamina to do the things you want, when you want. This means that health—specifically, your immune system—is a key factor in supporting you. We all know that it's no fun to feel crummy. It makes everything more difficult and it takes up too much energy. A sure-fire way to boost your immune system is to load up with antioxidants. You can do this with natural foods or with supplements. A few of my favorites are: JuicePlus+ (capsules and chewables), Sambucol Elderberry extract, Wellness Formula (capsules or liquid), Heathforce's Vitamineral Green powder, kale, spinach, kiwis, lemon, ginger, and cinnamon.

TASTE ME notes

DEBORAH KAGAN

~HIPPOCRATES

"A wise man should consider that health is the greatest of human blessings, and learn how by his own thought to derive benefit from his illnesses."

#14

How Sweet It Is

Don't you love that phrase, "the taste of success"? Whether you have something you love to eat or are simply eating to keep your engine running, you can turn the state of success around in your life by tasting LIFE in a new way. Get curious about what you're feeding yourself mentally, emotionally, spiritually and physically. Decipher what's "nutrient rich" and put that on the high-intake list. Moan when you eat something particularly delish. It changes the vibration of your body and amps it up. Yummo! Life is worth taking a big ol' bite out of. So go on—grab something that makes you swoon!

DEBORAH KAGAN

TASTE ME notes

~THEODORE WEISS

"Be in touch with excellence. Don't get lost in your own moods; they wear out too easily."

Shake It Up

Trying new things can be scary at times and even awkward—or it can be a total thrill. One of my heroes is Anthony Bourdain, world traveler/chef extraordinaire. He globetrots to the most unique, eccentric places solely to eat new, weird, wild and bizarre things. It's always an adventure and it always lights up his verve for life. Now, I'm not suggesting you go out and eat rattlesnake intestines (but by all means, don't let me stop you!). What I *am* suggesting is that you try something new. Remember the scene in *Pretty Woman* when she tries fine dining? She felt completely out of place but gave it a go and, even though the escargot flew across the table, it perked everyone up and energized the group.

Step out of your usual food intake. Try a new restaurant. Experiment with a new recipe. Explore a new culture's staple food. If you keep an open mind, you might find a pinch of fun creeps in.

TASTE ME notes

~TACITUS
"The desire for safety stands against every great and noble enterprise."

#16

Butter Me Up

A super-fun way to perk things up is to incorporate sex toys into your repertoire. These days they come in all shapes, sizes, colors, textures and TASTES! You can surprise your lover with a special tingle by using a mint-flavored lubricant. Sweetening things up is a cinch with all sorts of fruit-flavored lubes…and then there's the modern take on an old standard—candy necklaces. Only they've now turned the necklaces into pasties, panties and bra tops! Think about how excited your lover will be when you present him (or her) with the "challenge" of uncovering your delicacies one candy at a time!

A word of caution: If you are a woman prone to vaginal infections, do not insert any products that contain sugar or synthetics inside your vagina. Save those products for exterior use only. A wonderful all-natural product I frequently recommend for tasty fun is Sex Butter. You can find out all about it here: http://www.sex-butter.net

TASTE ME notes

~MARLENE DIETRICH
"In America sex is an obsession,
in other parts of the world it is a fact."

FIND YOUR ME SPOT

#17

Chocolate: 'Nuff Said

It's a rare occasion that I meet a woman who doesn't like chocolate. The good news is there are many conclusive studies that show multiple health benefits of chocolate. Two of the main ones are heart health and mood enhancement for both body and mind.

> Chocolate is a plentiful source of antioxidants. These are substances that reduce the ongoing cellular and arterial damage caused by oxidative reactions.
>
> You may have heard of a type of antioxidants called polyphenols. These are protective chemicals found in plant foods such as red wine and green tea. Chocolate, it turns out, is particularly rich in polyphenols. According to researchers at the University of Texas Southwestern Medical Center in Dallas, the same antioxidant properties found in red wine that protect against heart disease are also found in comparable quantities in chocolate.
>
> -—John Robbins. "Chocolate's Startling Health Benefits." huffingtonpost.com. February 2, 2011.

When you're feeling the need for a quick turn-on, reach out for some dark chocolate. Less than an ounce is all you need to pipe up a dull day. A few of my favorite kinds are:

Voges Chocolates: *Wooloomooloo, Organic Enchanted Mushroom* or *Barcelona*

Chocolove: *Almonds & Sea Salt* or *Chiles & Cherries*

Dagoba: *New Moon, Superfruit, Lavender Blueberry, Mint, Roseberry*

TASTE ME notes

~AUDREY HEPBURN

"Let's face it, a nice creamy chocolate cake does a lot for a lot of people; it does for me."

#18

Get Messy

Let's get primitive! The western world cleaned up the eating experience with utensils. It's removed us from feeling the nuances of our food.

ACTION

Eat with your hands!

Texture can enliven, entice and excite us. It perks up our fingertips, which are erogenous in nature. It also forces us to lick, suck and delight in our food with new perspective. Imagine what your morning oatmeal feels like. Imagine what spaghetti with tomato sauce feels like. Imagine what mixed green salad feels like. When you eat with your fingers, you're forced to slow down and really taste your food. It takes on new meaning and you can pretend you're Kim Basinger in *9 ½ Weeks!*

TASTE ME notes

~T.S. ELIOT
"Only those who will risk going too far
can possibly find out how far they can go."

#19

Say "Ahhhhhh"

A super-sexy, highly stimulating thing is to eat blindfolded. Yup. It's a little kinky and a lot hot! The cool thing about this is you're depriving one of your main senses (sight) usually linked to your food experience. This forces your taste buds to go into overdrive…and instantly makes you feel like a sensual being.

ACTION

Next meal you have, get a scarf and tie it around your head to cover your eyes. Do this alone or with your lover.

TASTE ME notes

~VOLTAIRE
"It is not love that should be depicted as blind, but self-love."

#20

Spice It Up!

Lighting up your insides is easy when you incorporate spices and flavors that naturally create more energy flow in your body. A few of my favorites are ginger, cinnamon, chile peppers and dark chocolate. Those are only a few. Many exotic spices are readily available in grocery stores these days. Next time you're shopping, pick out a few you've never tried and prepare a dish with them. The adventure of trying something new sparks your mojo.

TASTE ME notes

~ERMA BOMBECK

"Once you get a spice in your home, you have it forever. Women never throw out spices. The Egyptians were buried with their spices. I know which one I'm taking with me when I go."

#21

Breath of Life, Part I

Taste the breath of your life. Breathe. Intentionally. Most of the time we forget it's happening. Our body takes care of it for us. However, when we consciously take some SLOW DEEP BREATHS we are sending a message to our body that we are all right. We lower blood pressure, calm the nervous system, open the mind and activate our *power center*. This simple, profound gesture will keep you clear on what you really want to eat, say or do.

Take a few moments to get grounded in what's really true. Your breath is one of the most delicious things you "eat" on a daily basis. Enjoy it!

TASTE ME notes

~PEMA CHODRON

"It's also helpful to realize that this very body that we have, that's sitting right here right now... with its aches and it pleasures... is exactly what we need to be fully human, fully awake, fully alive."

Section Three

TOUCH ME

Sense-sational Facts

You have more pain nerve endings than any other type.

The least sensitive part of your body is the middle of your back.

The most sensitive areas of your body are your hands, lips, face, neck, tongue, fingertips and feet.

Shivering is a way your body has of trying to get warmer.

There are about 100 touch receptors in each of your fingertips.

Rattlesnakes use their skin to feel the body heat of other animals.

Touch ME

Your sense of touch is unique because, unlike the other four senses that are located in specific parts of your body, touch incorporates your entire body. It originates from the deepest layer of your skin, which is filled with many tiny nerve endings that carry the information to your brain via the spinal cord. Some areas of your body are more sensitive than others because they have more nerve endings.

What you put against your skin each and every day will not only affect your mood, it will determine how you feel about yourself. Frankly, if I lived in a colder climate I'd be swathed in the finest cashmere every day! Instead, I keep a cashmere wrap nearby at all times to remind me of the richness life has to offer.

Your fingertips are profoundly powerful and pick up information every second. Touch things that please you—always.

#22

The Fabric of Your Life

How does it feel when you're lying in bed?

Is your couch comfortable?

How do your feet feel when they touch the floor?

The fabrics in your home can enliven or deplete you. Surround yourself with sensuous fabrics. Decorative pillows in velvet, satin or fur are excellent and easy ways to amp up a room. Put a flokati rug under your desk and run your toes through it while you work. Toss a cashmere throw blanket over the side of your couch and lean up against it when you read a good book. Use silk pillowcases in bed and luxuriate in the cool, sexy sensation as you drift off to sleep. Cover your mattress in high-thread-count sheets just because they feel good against your skin.

DEBORAH KAGAN

TOUCH ME notes

~JOYCE MAYNARD
"A good home must be made, not bought."

#23 Royal Robes

Adornment is a key bonus about being a woman. From the beginning of time, women have prepared special outfits for certain occasions. Queens had garments made of the finest cloth and the most precious of jewels… and even their bedclothes were created for their pleasure. Fast-forward to modern day life, where we have the juggernaut of the fashion industry. EVERY woman has the option to dress like *her* version of a Queen.

You know when an outfit simply doesn't feel right. It can tweak your entire day and bring about a mood more foul than the dreaded monthly three-letter-word syndrome. That's because WHAT we wear makes a profound difference in how we encounter our day.

- The swish of a silk garment on your body can refresh you throughout the day.
- The snuggle of a cashmere sweater can stimulate healthy, safe emotions.
- The cool crispness of cotton pieces can inspire expansive thinking.

And let's not forget that—no matter what's going on—when you put on a great pair of shoes you can be invincible!

TOUCH ME notes

~GILDA RADNER

"I base my fashion taste on what doesn't itch."

#24 Animal Magnetism

One of my life's simple pleasures is taking a snuggle with Sage and Spirit, my cats. They don't enjoy a threesome snuggle but they are willing to indulge me in a one-to-one. Petting their soft coat, feeling the vibration of their purrrrrrr against my skin, instantly calms me.

Carin Gorrell writes in *Psychology Today*:

> Taking care of a loved one includes taking care of your pet. But here's something more to chew on: our pets take care of us in return. In fact, the man-and-his-dog bond can improve pet owners' physical and mental health. Pet ownership can have specific healing effects, including lower blood pressure and cholesterol levels. One study, from the University of New England in Australia, found that cat owners had fewer psychiatric disturbances than those without feline friends. And research conducted at the University of New York at Buffalo found that hypertensive stockbrokers improved dramatically after owning a pet for six months.

In addition to all the healing benefits, pets are an intricate piece of living a turned-on life because they are terrific intimacy partners. Try sitting with your pet, feeling its fur, and then synchronize your breathing with him or her. You can look into your pet's eyes as well. Notice the moment when you feel something click. This is when your soul connects to theirs, and vice versa. If you find it scary, weird or too vulnerable to be intimate with people in your life, practicing this technique with your pets is a great way to flex the intimacy muscle and build your confidence.

TOUCH ME notes

~ELEANOR H. PORTER

"It's funny how dogs and cats know the inside of folks better than other folks do, isn't it?"

#25
The Love Body Wash

The greatest way to feel loved, desired and worthy is through human touch. You have tremendous power in your hands, as do all people. A kind touch on someone's shoulder can change the landscape of his or her day. A hug can mean the world to someone. How you can give this to yourself is through *conscious body wash,* a tool I use and share with clients all the time. It transforms the way you feel about yourself, gives you more confidence and supports vibrant health. All you need is YOU!

Next time you take a bath or shower, you'll soap yourself up and clean off as usual…EXCEPT you'll say loving, appreciative things to yourself. For example:

- "Oh my! I LOVE my legs. They are strong, powerful and carry me throughout the day. My legs are AMAZING!"
- "Look how cute my toes are! WOW! I adore my toes and feet. They're so cool and they help me stand up all day, they take me places and I get to put pretty colors on the nails! My toes are AWESOME!"
- "Holy tumminess! Yum! I LOVE my belly. It's so sweet and soft. I'm super-grateful that right underneath this skin my tummy digests my food and keeps me nourished and healthy! My tummy is FABULOUS!"
- "Check out my arms! They're so strong and nurturing. I can wrap them around loved ones to hug them; they carry my purse and bags. They're super DELISH!"

You get the idea. The Love Body Wash is BIG, BOLD and UNABASHEDLY over the top. You need to make it this way to flip your switch. The combination of your words and touching your body at the same time wakes up all your cells, giving you sparkly energy for the day.

TOUCH ME notes

~HENRY DAVID THOREAU
"I stand in awe of my body."

#26

Touchy Feely

There have been hundreds of studies done on the healing power of touch. Conclusive results state that touch can calm anxiety, make you more alert, lessen symptoms of depression, fatigue, or irritability, and decrease chronic illness and disease. PLUS, when you are touched by another human it reminds you how delightful it is to be in a human body.

There are many therapies and opportunities to incorporate human touch into your life. Here are a few of my favorite:

MASSAGE: This is one of the more traditional ways to experience human touch. There are variations in types of massage such as Swedish, Deep Tissue, Lymph-o-massage, Thai, Hot Stone, and so on.

HANDS-ON HEALING: These sessions are becoming more en vogue as of the last decade. Different types of healing are Reiki, Heller work and Rolfing.

SEXOLOGICAL BODYWORK: Relatively new to mainstream life, sexological bodywork is a powerful way to experience safe touch. Sessions can include a variety of educational modalities such as breathwork, conscious movement, touch, erotic massage, pelvic release bodywork, scar tissue remediation, and Orgasmic Yoga coaching.

DEBORAH KAGAN

TOUCH ME notes

~SHAKTI GAWAIN

"I am convinced that life in a physical body is meant to be an ecstatic experience."

#27

Make Out With Nature, Part 1

I admit it. I'm a tree hugger! It seriously feels SO GOOD. Whenever there's a need to spark my mojo I go for a straight shot (no chaser) of nature. When we spend time in nature we are literally making a connection with everything. We are giving ourselves a moment to slow down, feel what's really going on and wipe away the fog of our emotional selves. You ever notice that you get the most profound ideas when you're out for that jog, hike or long walk?

Get out, get connected, and feel some SOIL beneath your feet. Get on the earth and let her give you strength, clarity and wisdom.

Shake hands with the shrubs, plants and flowers outside your home. They each have their own personalities (spiky, smooth, sticky…). Get to know them!

Wrap your arms around a tree. Feel its trunk pressing up against you and its roots below you. Take a few deep breaths and see what she's got to say. You'll be surprised at all the ancient information available to you.

DEBORAH KAGAN

TOUCH ME notes

~ARISTOTLE
"In all things of nature there is something of the marvelous."

#28
Little Shop of Lovelies

Every woman loves a little sumptin' sumptin' sexy to put on under her clothes. Maybe you enjoy cotton delicacies. Maybe silk. Maybe you're in discovery mode about your lingerie go-to choice. Whatever strikes your fancy, there's one outing you must go on at least once a year to tickle your turn-on—*visiting a high-end lingerie shop*. I'm not talking Victoria's Secret here (though they're great for more day-to-day fun). I mean the lingerie shop that carries foreign brands, little particulars and unmentionables that cost more than a week's worth of groceries.

You don't need to purchase anything. The point to visiting these shops is that it opens your mind to new ideas and possibilities. It plunks you square down in the midst of where people go to initiate a turn-on of some kind—and that, in turn, will spark yours.

Feel the fabrics. Let your fingers do the talking. Imagine which pieces you'd enjoy wearing. Try one or two on for reference. Go with a friend if that makes it easier. No matter what, treat this as the sexy excursion that it is and have fun with it!

TOUCH ME notes

~DOROTHY PARKER
"Brevity is the soul of lingerie."

#29

Flip Your Wig

Have you ever noticed how every woman's hair texture is slightly different? Curly hair is generally more coarse and porous. Straight hair is generally more silky and smooth. We are born with our unique texture and we are used to it. It's what we know. Some of us love our locks and others spend endless hours and countless amounts of money on products and services to make it look or feel a certain way. The cool thing is that women can temporarily change the feel of their hair in numerous ways.

One of the easiest (and most fun!) is with a wig. You'll not only get a new feel; you'll get a new look as well. Plus, you can take it right off so there's no fear of how long will you have to live with it.

The first time I bought a wig, I wanted the exact opposite of my own curly, rough hair. I bought a straight, chin length bob with bangs. It was sassy. I loved the feel of bangs kissing my forehead. I could run my fingers ALL the way through the hair. It was so unique and sexy. I noticed my walk and posture changed. I felt like a heightened version of myself. And I couldn't stop touching my hair! It was so fun.

What kind of hair have you always wanted to try on? Go to your local wig store (or do an internet search), try it on…and find out what part of your personality pops up.

DEBORAH KAGAN

TOUCH ME notes

~HENRY ROD
"Whether you believe you can do
a thing or not, you are right."

#30

Plant Cosmic Seeds

Take out a journal, a scratchpad, an iPad or any other tool you like, and record your goals. These words are the seeds you're planting with the intention to make them grow. You're literally putting an order into the cosmic garden.

Next, make a realistic action list and stick to it for the next two weeks. Take a measurable step every day towards each of the goals you've set forth. These are the seeds you plant in the garden of your life. And if you're anything like me, you'll appreciate the reminder a friend consistently gives me when I start to get impatient if I don't see "results" ASAP: when you seed the lawn for grass and go out the next day screaming "Where's the grass?!", you're setting yourself up for disappointment. Plant your seeds and know without a shadow of a doubt they are growing. A lot happens underground before you ever see a sprout!

TOUCH ME notes

~B.C. FORBES

"One worthwhile task carried to a successful conclusion is worth half a hundred half-finished tasks."

#31

Truth Serum Letters

You know when you go to those family gatherings and you get choked up? Not because you're feeling all emotionally warm and gooey. I mean the kind of choked up when you want to choke the other person for all the silly, stupid stuff they've done but you just can't let that cat out of the bag—cuz it's family. These are the times where you want to go old school and take out some paper and pen. Get TACTILE.

Plop yourself down in a quiet corner and have at it with the page. Write down ALL the things you've wanted to say to this person. Doesn't have to be nice, make sense or be any sort of cohesive. This is your time to spew everything. Write it out. Cry, stomp, laugh—just get it out. When you feel empty, take the page and either burn it or bury it outside. You'll be pleasantly amazed at how free you'll feel.

On the flip side, writing yourself a love letter is another fabulous way to use your hands with pen and paper. Write down all the things you want to hear. How wonderful you are. How you're worthy of beauty, abundance, peace, joy, love, brilliant health and a stimulating intimate partner. Use all the words you imagine someone would say to you if they were fulfilling your utmost fantasy. Spell it all out for yourself. When complete, you can tuck it away in a special box, place it under your mattress or plant it outside in the earth's soil.

TOUCH ME notes

~RUFUS M. JONES

"Serenity comes not alone by removing the outward causes and occasions of fear, but by the discovery of inward reservoirs to draw upon."

Section Four

HEAR
ME

Sense-sational Facts

Babies can get earaches because of milk backing up in the Eustachian tube, which causes bacteria to grow and may cause hearing problems later in life.

When you go up to high elevations, the change in pressure causes your ears to pop.

Children have more sensitive ears than adults. They can recognize a wider variety of noises.

Dolphins have the best sense of hearing among animals. They are able to hear 14 times better than humans.

Animals hear more sounds than humans.

An earache is caused by too much fluid putting pressure on your eardrum. Earaches are often the result of an infection, allergies or a virus.

Hear ME

Your ears are extremely well-designed. They serve two key purposes: to hear sounds and help keep your balance. When you hear things, you are actually connecting to vibrations known as sound waves. These vibrations are channeled through the complex system of your ear, ultimately landing in your brain to make sense of the information.

What you put in your ears each and every day will not only affect how you feel about yourself, it will determine what you feel you are capable of doing or being. Your ears hear literal (voices, nature, news, music, construction, etc.) and figurative (inner thoughts) things 24/7. When they're downloading negative information, you'll feel bad, afraid and small. When they're downloading positive information, you'll feel fabulous, confident and powerful. Seek out the sounds that bring the most harmony to who you choose to BE and where you intend to GO.

FIND YOUR ME SPOT

#32

Funk!

As in George Clinton and the Parliament Funkadelic. Turn on some tunes and work your funky MOJO! Pick whatever inspires you and let it wiggle its way into your ear canal. Music gives us the incredible gift of emotion. A certain song can inspire, tug on your heartstrings, pump you up, or even irritate you.

One of my favorite things about music is that it gives you permission to move your body. Dancing, groovin' or any semblance of that will hands-down shake the turn-on into you. It's biologically impossible to stay in the same state of being when you move your body. So get to it! Press play on your iTunes mix and shake that booty. If you add a smile on your face, you get extra turn-on points.

BONUS!

Here's access to three of my personal favorite playlists for working the mojo: www.findyourmespotbook.com

DEBORAH KAGAN

HEAR ME notes

~RAY CHARLES

"I was born with music inside me. Music was one of my parts. Like my ribs, my kidneys, my liver, my heart. Like my blood. It was a force already within me when I arrived on the scene. It was a necessity for me-like food or water."

#33
The Call of the Wild

Some people enjoy the sounds of crashing waves. Some, the light dance of rain falling on the earth. Others enjoy the coo of birds calling their tribe or the orchestral nuances of a rain forest or a hot summer night or even a heartbeat.

With life moving über fast, we've become more and more distanced from the rhythms of the earth. So, it's no surprise that sound machines with various nature options have become popular this century. Whether you connect with the real deal or use a facsimile, allow nature's songs to engorge your eardrums. Not only will you feel more grounded; you'll also have a deeper connection to your own innate pace.

DEBORAH KAGAN

HEAR ME notes

~ARISTOTLE
"Nature does nothing uselessly."

#34
Your "Once Upon a Time"

What are you telling yourself every day? I'm talking about mindset here, folks. What are those thoughts, beliefs and mental gymnastics that hold your attention? I can guarantee—they are NOT THE TRUTH. You need to look at what's really running your life. Unfortunately, the majority of us out there are tuned into an outdated radio station that plays only static.

One tool I use and recommend is identifying your "characters." These are the different roles you play in life. For instance, your personal character is slightly different from your professional character. You also have certain interests or hobbies that bring out other facets of your personality. Each of these characters has specific wisdom as well as distinct strengths. Their voices are unique and they tell you things you need to know.

There's a template I use to teach my clients about identifying and working with their characters (you can find out more here: http://www.deborah-kagan.com/mojomakeover). You need to know about them because when you access these characters, you become much more confidant in who you are.

When you are in communication with your characters, you have control over their voices. This puts the right DJ in charge of your inner radio station.

HEAR ME notes

~HORACE
"Force without wisdom falls of its own weight."

#35

Solo Sexy Time

Ladies, I know we talked about this before—but this is très important and bears repeating. Regardless if you're in a relationship or not, taking some ME time is the KEY to staying sane and healthy. Even if you've got all your extended family visiting from Timbuktu and you're not going to see them again for 10 years. You've got to give yourself at least FIVE MINUTES of what I call "Stop. Look. Listen." Stop to actually look at yourself. For real. In the mirror. Look into your eyes. Breathe. Who's looking back at you? Not the skin and bones person. The other one, the one behind your eyes. Who's that? **Listen to that person.** They're the one with the truth. They're the one who knows you're sexy because you're so insatiably YOU. They're the one that wants you to put on the feather boa for the holiday party and line your eyes with the glitter. Go on and take a look. You'll be met with a love you might not have known was actually living IN you this whole time.

DEBORAH KAGAN

HEAR ME notes

~MARK RUTHERFORD

"There is in each of us an upwelling spring of life, energy, love,
whatever you like to call it. If a course is not cut for it,
it turns the ground around it into a swamp."

#36

Mix It Up

You cannot live a turned-on life when you are holing up and playing the role of "yogi on mountaintop." As a wise woman once said to me, "You've got to get out of the house." With the overwhelming amount of technology used these days, we are drifting farther and farther apart from REAL connection. Get out. Have conversations that are longer than 140 characters and actually occur with your MOUTH and not your fingertips. When you do, you'll find out you've got a lot to say and people will guide you to where you need to be. All you need to do is talk with them and be interested in what they have to say. The rest will happen.

ACTION

While you're out in the world today, strike up a conversation with a new person. One of the best ways to do this is to give compliments. It forces you to pay attention to details and engage in all of your senses.

HEAR ME notes

~RUFUS M. JONES
"Serenity comes not alone by removing the outward causes and occasions of fear, but by the discovery of inward reservoirs to draw upon."

#37
Curiosity Didn't Kill the Cat

Wanna know why? Because the more you inquire, the more you know. And the more you know, the better decisions you can make. And when you make decisions, your life grows exponentially into the direction of your goals and dreams. Be curious about your life and, even more importantly, be curious about other people's lives. We get the most amazing clues from other people. You know when you have the "random" conversation in the coffee shop and amidst the "wow, it's a crazy day, huh?" a morsel of genius can pop up for either one of you? Ask questions all the time! Be open to what you hear in the answers.

HEAR ME notes

~VICTOR HUGO
"Curiosity is one of the forms of feminine bravery."

#38

Noise Pollution

You spend your entire day listening to information. The sounds and thoughts moving through your ears every day have a profound effect, not only on how you view your life but also on how you view yourself.

TV, media, radio, books on tape, mp3s, conferences and classes you listen to all vie for your attention. Are they enhancing the quality of your life? Or do they instill fear and worry?

Regarding the news, best-selling author and New Thought minister Mary Morrissey said it best: CNN stands for Constantly Negative News.

WHO you listen to, WHAT you listen to and WHERE you position yourself to gather information are all crucial to your success. Especially while you are recalibrating and in the process of finding your "me spot," be fiercely protective of what you allow to penetrate your ear canal. All Sensually Empowered Women come to this knowledge. Hopefully it's sooner rather than later.

DEBORAH KAGAN

HEAR ME notes

~GLORIA STEINEM
"The first problem for all of us, men and women, is not to learn, but to unlearn."

#39

Hear Ye, Hear Ye

Opt for a "hearing meditation." The ancient Tantric Yogis utilize this technique to sharpen their senses and become more engaged in life. When you take the time to isolate one sense, it forces you to become more aware of your immediate surroundings and heightens everything in your vicinity.

A sexy way to do this is get a blindfold. You can use an actual one or take a silk scarf, your eye mask for sleeping…or a man's tie is always a fun option. Tie the blindfold around your head securely enough to block out any light or images. Now sit or lie comfortably in a room where you won't be disturbed. This isn't like other meditations where you listen to your breath. What you want to do is get hyper-connected to the sounds around you. Maybe your breath is one of the sounds. Can you hear the wind outside? Are there people walking around in the next room? Can you hear a squirrel running up the tree? Is the hot water heater clanking? A plane flying overhead? Was that a fly buzzing in the window screen? Your only job is to listen. When your brain starts having a conversation about the sounds, and how that one reminds you that you need to buy more toilet paper, take a breath and dial all your attention back to your ears and sound. What do you hear? Let the utter subtlety of sound amaze you or let the cacophony of sounds bowl you over.

Stay engaged in this listening meditation for a minimum of three minutes.

DEBORAH KAGAN

HEAR ME notes

~VIRGIL
"Every sound alarms."

#40

Body Talk

Listen Up. To your body. Yes. I said listen to your body. It tells you EVERYTHING. It knows what you REALLY want to eat. It knows when you REALLY need to sleep...and with whom you REALLY want to sleep (I mean in the s-e-x version of sleep). It knows when something's off, when you need to see a doctor or specialist. It knows all your secrets and, if you've buried them, your body can bring them up when you least expect. Your body is your ally. Get acquainted, have a cup o' sumptin' with it and learn to dialogue. The relationship you have with your body is the longest one you'll ever have. It comes with you from birth to death. Your body is exquisite.

⚡ MOJO TIP

When conversing with your body, tune in and start to understand when your body feels expansive and when it's contracting. The opening, expansive feeling is your body telling you YES! The contraction is an indication to ask more questions, dig deeper...or it's a plain ol' NO!

HEAR ME notes

~HENRY MILLER
"Our own physical body possesses a wisdom which we who inhabit the body lack."

#41
Talk to Me, Baby

There are five keys to your storehouse of personal magnetism. One of them is your tone of voice. Your voice speaks volumes about who you are, what energy is flowing (or not) in your body, and how available you are for personal interaction.

One of the best ways to amp up your turn-on is to play with your voice. There's the tone of voice we use for most of our day. This could be your work/professional voice, or maybe it's your mom voice. That's merely one aspect of what you're capable of and who you are. When you want to inspire your lover, your daily voice is not the one that's guaranteed to light them up. Becoming adept at knowing when to use what tone, and with whom, is a powerful skill to possess. Your voice can inspire people to come toward you as easily as it can repel them. It can command a room or not. Learning how to modulate your voice will bring out more of your essence. Since we're talking specifically about your turned-on life, here's a way to dial up your sensuality:

Slow. Your. Voice. Down. Sloooooow. Iiiiiiiiiiiit. Waaaaaaaaay. Dowwwwwwwwwn.

It will seem weird and probably absurd at first. That's why it's a good idea to do this alone. When you slow your voice down, your entire throat relaxes. It gets loose and breathy. Like Marilyn Monroe. In fact, practice talking like Marilyn five minutes a day for a week straight. There's nothing like it to integrate the sultry flavor into your life.

DEBORAH KAGAN

HEAR ME notes

~AIMEE MULLINS
"Confidence is the sexiest thing a woman can have.
It's much sexier than any body part."

#42 Adult Story Time

When was the last time you read an erotic novel? Never? Well, my friend, here's your assignment. Go get an erotic book, story or article. You can find oodles of them online or in your local bookstore. A few of my favorites are listed here: www.findyourmespotbook.com

This is Wikipedia's definition:

> **Erotica** (from the Greek ἔρως, eros—"desire") are works of art, including literature, photography, film, sculpture and painting, that deal substantively with erotically stimulating or sexually arousing descriptions.

When we want a quick turn-on fix, reading erotica OUT LOUD is a fun, sassy way to do it. Read it to yourself before bed. Read it aloud to yourself in the bath. Read it to your lover. Read it to your pet. Just get to reading it aloud. Hear those words come out of your mouth. How does your body feel speaking them? Are you nervous? It is comfortable? Does it seem silly?

Sensually Empowered Women know the power of this language. Try it on and give yourself permission to play with the erotic woman that's inside you. I know she's there!

HEAR ME notes

~ISABEL ALLENDE

"Erotica is using a feather,
pornography is using the whole chicken."

Section Five

SMELL
ME

Sense-sational Facts

Dogs have 1 million smell cells per nostril and their smell cells are 100 times larger than humans!

Humans use insect warning chemicals, called pheromones, to keep away pesky insects.

People who cannot smell have a condition called Anosmia.

If your nose is at its best, you can tell the difference between 4000-10,000 smells!

As you get older, your sense of smell gets worse. Children are more likely to have better senses of smell than their parents or grandparents.

Smell ME

Your nose is the gateway for the tiny, imperceptible odor particles floating through the environment (aka smells) to reach your olfactory system, which then sends signals to your brain to decode the smells. Because our sense of smell is connected to our memory, its effects are palpable.

What you put under your nose each and every day will not only affect your emotional state, it will influence the decisions you make. Everyone has her favorite smells, scents that remind her of something sweet and special. On the flip side, there are smells that dredge up icky, uncomfortable experiences. Our olfactory system is the one part of our sensory nature that connects the dots between past, present and future. Choose to surround yourself with the literal and figurative scents that support your ideal life, not the ones you simply tolerate.

#43

Truth or BS?

Literally and figuratively, you can smell a "rat" when it's there. You know when you're BS-ing and when you're allowing the TRUTH to unfold. One of the most powerful things a woman can do is get real with herself. It not only supports creating an authentic life, it dramatically increases awareness of what's comfortable and what's not.

Women, inherently, are people pleasers. In theory, that's kind and generous. In reality, it leads to us doing things we don't want to do, going places we'd rather not and leaving our desires on a low flame way way WAY on the back of life's proverbial burner.

And here's the rub: *there's never a good time to pipe up and call yourself on the sham*. There's always an excuse to be found, a "reason" that seems bigger and more important to breathe life into. The truth is—living like that keeps you stuck. It's disempowering.

Try this on for size next time you're at the BS crossroads:

Wherever you are, stop whatever it is that you're doing and take a deep whiff of the air around you. Inhale so the breath reaches your belly. As you exhale, notice if your body relaxes. Do your muscles peel away from the bones? Does your jaw loosen up? Do you have a sense of expansion in your body? If yes, then you're on the right track. If no, there's something you're kidding yourself about. Do you *really* want to go out for Chinese tonight? If not, you can simply redirect your energy, share your truth ("You know, I'm feeling more like staying in. I'd enjoy ordering delivery.") and watch your life become more and more consistent moments of existing in your ME spot.

DEBORAH KAGAN

SMELL ME notes

~INDIRA GANDHI
"You cannot shake hands with a clenched fist."

#44 Playing With Fire

If you are one of those people who wants to save candle lighting for a "special" occasion, remember: there is no more special occasion than you being alive today! Spark up the candles. There are incredible aromatherapy candles available in every scent, for every mood and all occasions. It's important to be discerning about the candles you do burn because they become a key ingredient in your environmental health.

Soy or pure beeswax candles are the cleanest ones on the market. Make sure to keep your wicks trimmed down. Longer wicks produce more soot and take away from the therapeutic properties of the aromatherapy candle.

A saucy way to spice up your love life is to use massage candles. These are the kind that when they burn, the wax turns into massage oil. You simply pour it over your lover (or they pour it on you). It's warm, sexy and smells divine!

So ladies, get out the aromatherapy candles, put them in all rooms of your home and light 'em up. Not only is it super-cozy and sexy, it'll bring more heat chi lighting up your mojo.

SMELL ME notes

~JODY WATLEY

"I'll put candles all over the room, then light them, and get to it. I call it my 'vibe in a bag.'"

#45

Smoke Signals

One of my favorite ways to incorporate smell is with incense. Incense has been used for hundreds of years for rituals, purification ceremonies, meditation, mood enhancing and of course for masking foul odors. Most people think about frankincense and myrrh when thinking of incense. However, the variety of incense available today is vast.

Lighting a stick of incense radically shifts the energy of a room. Many ancient cultures believe there's a spirit within the incense and, by lighting it, you activate the spiritual force of the plants, resins and natural elements that are the ingredients of the incense. Therefore, it's considered bad luck to blow out the flame with your breath. Instead, wave the stick from side to side or up and down to extinguish the flame.

A simple daily ritual can be made out of lighting a stick of incense. It is an effective tool for keeping in touch with your 6th sense. Choose a flavor you enjoy and a burner that suits your décor. I found a gorgeous deco glass shallow bowl in the shape of an elongated leaf once. If you choose to use a conventional bowl or dish as opposed to a traditional incense burner, the trick is to fill the dish with a substance that will support the incense standing up. Rice, sand or moist clay are all good options.

When you light the incense, take a moment to set an intention. Maybe it's one for the hour, day or month. Acknowledge that the smoke will carry your desire into the world to make the message loud and clear.

DEBORAH KAGAN

SMELL ME notes

~PABLO PICASSO
"Everything you can imagine is real."

#46

Bodacious Blooms

Women love beauty. It's innate to the feminine. One of the easiest ways to bring beauty into your life is with fresh flowers. It's also a fabulous way to transform a room with smell. Think about all the fancy hotels and restaurants. They always have a gorgeous arrangement of flowers in the main area. It's visually pleasing and adds exciting fragrance to the space.

Flowers don't need to be expensive, either. Farmer's markets are excellent places to pick up incredibly lush flowers, as are corner markets in most towns. Remember, not every flower has a strong fragrance, so pick ones that perk up your olfactory system.

 **MOJO TIP**

To powerfully bring new opportunities, fresh energy and more abundance into your life, perform the flower ritual. Buy some fragrant flowers. Place them in the main room of your home of office. Do this again three days later (if you buy them on Monday, you'll buy some more on Thursday). Repeat this process consecutively every three days for a total of nine times.

DEBORAH KAGAN

SMELL ME notes

~RALPH WALDO EMERSON
"Earth laughs in flowers."

FIND YOUR ME SPOT

#47

Calgon, Take Me Away

Everyone has to bathe at least a few times a week…at least we hope they do! It's a mundane part of life that can be glossed over and left for rote. When you choose to transform your bathing ritual into one of sensual pleasure, you'll find new ways to enjoy more energy, enthusiasm and excitement for life.

It's incredibly easy for women to incorporate the sense of smell into bathing. Think about all the items you use: shampoo, conditioner, face soap, body soap, salt scrubs, shaving lotion, body oil and more! Turn your bathroom into a place of aroma goodness and perk things up.

 MOJO TIP

Combine your favorite scents with the Love Body Wash (#25) for major mojo enhancement.

SMELL ME notes

~LAO-TZU

"(S)He who loves the world as (her)his body may be entrusted with the empire."

#48 Common Scents

Who says washing the dishes and doing laundry is a chore? These two things can be a joy when consciously incorporating certain smells to the task.

Go into your kitchen right now and smell your dish soap. Does it invigorate you? Or nauseate you? Is it chock-full of chemicals that make you think of an industrial factory? If so, go to the grocery store and seek out a pleasing dish soap. There's a plethora of options available. Frankly, I play a game when it's time to buy cleaning supplies. It's called the "what's going to make me happiest this time" game. Some weeks I'm in a citrus mood; others a calming mood. Every now and again I'm in a woodsy, nature mood.

The same goes for laundry supplies. Is there a particular smell that reminds you of comfort? Like when you were a kid and your mom did laundry? Maybe that smell gives you an emotional boost. Or maybe your life is a constant go, go, go and you could really use a reminder to relax. That's the time to toss a lavender dryer sheet in with your load.

When it comes to dishes and laundry, feel into what's going to light your fire, and go for it!

SMELL ME notes

~SOPHOCLES
"One learns by doing the thing; for though you think you know it, you have no certainty until you try."

#49 Scents and Sensibilities

It's no surprise that the perfume industry is a multi-billion dollar market. Every fashion magazine on the planet regularly features an article on perfumes, celebrities tout their signature scents and the dollars and cents spent on a bottle can indicate one's status.

Perfume or scented body oils make a statement about your personality. Ideally, your scent enhances you and doesn't overpower. Women have many flavors and facets depending on mood, time of month and companions. It's a good idea to find a few scents that rev up your mojo. Think about one for your professional life, one for your personal life and one that simply titillates you (in other words, makes you want to get down with yo' sensual self!).

Generally, perfumes can be boiled down to a handful of categories. The fruity personality tends to be outgoing, optimistic and enjoy pampering themselves. The Oriental is someone who leans towards exotic locales and experiences. They are generally passionate, powerful people. The Woody personality loves jetsetting, the ocean, fresh foods and a natural vibe. The Delicate personality enjoys sports and being a part of the crowd, and tends to go with the flow. The Sensual personality is confidant and a go-getter who appreciates the attention of the opposite sex.

 MOJO TIP

Make a date with yourself and head to the perfume counter. Sample a few scents until you find one that perks you up. Spritz it on and live with it for the rest of the day. The scent will change with your body chemistry. If you still like it at the end of the day, you've found a winner.

DEBORAH KAGAN

SMELL ME notes

~CHRISTIAN DIOR
"A woman's perfume tells more about her than her handwriting."

#50
Breath of Life, Part II

We spoke about this in Taste #21, however it's so effective that it bears repeating. Breathing. Most of the time we forget it's happening. Our body takes care of it for us. Our breath moves in and out of our nasal passages, exactly where we connect to our sense of smell. You're doing it right now even though you might have no awareness of it. However, when we consciously take some SLOW DEEP BREATHS we send a message to our body that we are all right. We lower blood pressure, calm the nervous system, open the mind and activate our "power center." This simple, profound gesture will keep you clear on what you really want to eat, say or do.

Today, take time before you make any decision to slow down and connect to your breath. Notice how it makes you feel. From here on out, let your breath become the barometer for your sense of well-being and confidence.

SMELL ME notes

~THICH NHAT HANH
"Feelings come and go like clouds in a windy sky.
Conscious breathing is my anchor."

#51 Make Out With Nature, Part II

Nature is a potent smell factory, and when we spend time in nature we are literally making a connection with everything. We are giving ourselves a moment to slow down, feel what's really going on and wipe away the fog of our emotional selves. You ever notice that you get the most profound ideas when you're out for that jog, hike or long walk? Get out, feel some SOIL beneath your feet. NOT concrete. Get on the earth and discover her scents. Are there wild herbs growing in your neighborhood? Have you stopped to smell your neighbor's roses? Does the dogwood tree or the pine bring a smile to your face?

No matter where you live, city or suburb, go find that piece of Mother Nature near you and let her give strength, clarity and wisdom to your day.

DEBORAH KAGAN

SMELL ME notes

~DANIEL WEBSTER

"The materials of wealth are in the earth, in the seas, and in their natural and unaided productions."

#52 Aromatherapy

Aromatherapy is an ancient tool. Used for centuries, it has been part of rituals, healing, skin care and a variety of home uses. It uses volatile plant materials, known as essential oils, combined with other aromatic compounds. These days, there are practitioners that specialize in aromatherapy to support people in altering their mind's mood, health and cognitive functioning.

I believe every home needs to have a few key essential oils in the medicine cabinet. I've listed them for you here with their corresponding uses. Take note: it's important to buy high quality, pure essential oils because they offer the strongest healing power and possess a high vibration frequency.

Lavender – stress relief, antidepressant, anti-inflammatory, sedative.

Tea Tree – immune booster, anti-fungal, insecticide, soothes cold sores and a sundry of other skin conditions.

Rosemary – mental stimulant, soothes cramping muscles, supports digestion, stimulates the scalp and hair growth.

Peppermint – alertness, energy boosting, digestive aid, breath freshener, alleviates congestion.

Rose – helps circulation, heart opening, diminishes anxiety, excellent for radiant skin.

Ylang Ylang – stress reducer, aphrodisiac, soothes headaches, romance enhancer.

Sandalwood – tension relief, calming, enhances sexual energy, anti-inflammatory.

Lemon – improves concentration, aids digestion, reduces acne, immune booster, quick mood enhancer.

Use the oils individually or get creative and make a blend to suit your needs.

Some ways to use the oils are:

- as an inhalant
- in a diffuser to burn in the home or office
- in the shower or bath
- as an aura cleanse*
- in body or massage oil

Aura Cleanse

Choose the oil (or oils) you want to use. Pour three drops into your LEFT palm. Take your RIGHT palm, place on top of the left and rub the right palm over left NINE times in a clockwise direction, blending the oil into the skin.

Clap palms together vigorously THREE times.

"Wash" your body with both hands as you wave them up your front side, down each arm, around the back and over the head without actually touching yourself. Make sure you also get down to your feet. The idea here is to clean your aura, which is the energy field around your physical body.

Once thoroughly cleaned, cup your palms in front of your nose and deeply inhale. Exhale with sound. Ahhhhhh. Repeat two more times.

FIND YOUR ME SPOT
SMELL ME notes

~MAYA ANGELOU
"Determine to live life with flair and laughter."

SMELL ME notes

~ALBERT EINSTEIN
"Look deep into nature, and then you will understand everything better."

Section Six

MORE, MORE, MORE!

#53

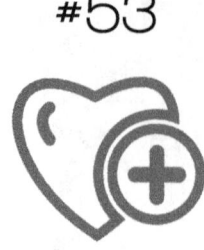

Your Date With Destiny

As you may realize at this point, I'm a big fan of ritual. Marking moments with consciousness allows for clarity in what we're creating. Whether you find it's the turning of another calendar year, a new month, a new week or a new or full moon, it's a good idea to reflect on what you've accomplished, where you are now and where you're going in the next phase.

Here's a plan for paving the way:

GET NAKED.

Take a blank (naked) sheet of paper and a pen you just dig. For three minutes write nonstop about all the things you've experienced in the last phase (week, month year, etc.). Write out all the milestones. What wins did you have? What losses? What excited you and made you giddy? What moments made your heart break? Once you've written it all out, take a deep belly breath. Scan the list. Let it sink into your consciousness and then move to the next step.

BURN, BABY, BURN.

After reviewing your list, see what qualities in yourself are associated with loss or with the events you felt didn't go as planned. Were you more stubborn than necessary? Did you let fear paralyze you more often than not?

Identify these main qualities you'd like to release, allowing you to therefore shift into the new cycle unencumbered. Write these qualities on a new piece of paper in any way you see fit. Then, hold the paper in your hand and close your eyes. See your body opening up little doors to release these qualities. Maybe they're coming out of your hips, your brain or your heart. Finally, give them permission to leave as you burn the paper.

WATCH ME GROW.

After the fire-releasing ritual, fill the room you've created in your consciousness with what you'd like to expand in the next phase. Maybe you'd like more patience or a new sense of gratitude day-to-day or to become more generous. Write these things down on a new piece of paper. Take it and either bury it in the ground outside your front door or in a potted plant inside your home. Allow the earth to swallow these psychic seeds, and trust they will grow in your life.

MAPPING THE COURSE.

We can get grandiose with setting goals. That's often the reason most people will fall short. Is it important for us to stretch? HELL YES! However, if you set a goal that you can't connect with sensorially then it's bound to pass you up. Get really clear on up to FIVE things you want to create in the next phase. Make sure you can feel, sense, taste, smell or see them ACTUALLY manifesting. When you set these five things, go slightly beyond what you feel is possible. Write them down and keep them in a special place (I put mine in a Chinese Red Envelope and keep it on my altar.). Then take measurable actions to achieve the goals and meet the universe as it rises up to offer them to you.

FIND YOUR ME SPOT

MORE, MORE, MORE notes

~KEN KESEY

"Ritual is necessary for us to know anything."

MORE, MORE, *MORE* notes

~TONY ROBBINS
"It is in your moments of decision that your destiny is shaped."

#54

Simon Says Stop

Seriously. Just stop. Stop doing, stop tweeting, stop racing, stop all the things that keep you whirling faster than the Tasmanian Devil. This is not an easy thing for women. Women like to be in motion because, at its core, feminine expression is constantly flowing without end. It craves sway, swoosh, life, light, glitter and shine. **For 5 minutes—do nothing.** Get quiet. See what's happening in the vast space that is the REAL you. You might be surprised at what's there to greet you.

MORE, MORE, *MORE* notes

DEBORAH KAGAN

~DR. JOYCE BROTHERS

"No matter how much pressure you feel at work, if you could find ways to relax for at least five minutes every hour, you'd be more productive."

#55

Ride the Waves

For all of you reading this who "hunker in," "buckle down" and "get through it"…STOP IT! All that does it create a hardened physical body that becomes more and more disassociated from the natural body's intelligence and your emotions. Go with your emotional flow. Let yourself really experience whatever you are feeling and, in the same moment, REMEMBER without a doubt that the emotions will pass. They are as fleeting as the weather AND we must give them room to move in our life. When we shut ourselves off to this innate flow, we block our life force and therefore our ability to be plugged in.

DEBORAH KAGAN

MORE, MORE, MORE notes

~ANNE SEXTON
"Oh, darling, let your body in, let it tie you in, in comfort."

#56

The Holy Trinity

The following three factors are instrumental facets to personal and professional growth:

FIND THE EXPERT.

When you want something done and you want it done right, find the person or people who do nothing but that thing. Guaranteed they get it done faster, with more efficiency and will ultimately save you loads of dough-rey-me. Why? Because if it's what they spend the majority of their time doing, they'll know the ins, outs, sideways and upside-downs of whatever it is. When you need your oil changed, you go to the mechanic. When your kitchen sink explodes, you call the plumber. When your home is keeping you from thriving, you bring in the Feng Shui consultant. All of these things might feel like higher up-front costs—but we all know that the big-picture payoff FAR outweighs the initial investment.

FIND YOUR CENTER OF THE UNIVERSE.

Life is crazy nutty. It's always going to be a wild ride with highs and lows and everything in between. That's why it's CRUCIAL to know what keeps you grounded. Everyone has something that brings them back into balance—the thing, place, person or experience that makes you breathe deeper. It's the one where you can literally feel your shoulders heading down your body and away from your ears. A few of mine are the ocean, a Steve Ross yoga class and hugging trees. Take the time to really figure out what you need to keep connected to your center. Then, no matter what happens, you can go to it and be reminded 'it's all good.'

FIND YOUR WOO-HOO! A big part of my success has been learning to celebrate. When we take time to pat ourselves on the back, we honor what we've done, which only encourages us to move forward for more. Celebrate ALL the things in your life—little and large. You don't have to go out and throw a champagne and caviar fest for every little thing (though that sounds like fun!). But you do need to be liberal with the self-kudos. A few ways I celebrate are: giving myself a standing ovation, taking an overnight mini-break or having a piece of really outstanding chocolate. However you choose to do it, make sure it feels good for you and that you really relish it in the moment

FIND YOUR ME SPOT

MORE, MORE, MORE notes

~TENNESSEE WILLIAMS
"Enthusiasm is the most important thing in life."

MORE, MORE, MORE notes

~SALLY KIRKLAND

"My attitude is always one of sensuality, aggressive enthusiasm and a kind of outrageousness in my expression"

#57

Girls' Club

This might come as a shocker, however…I didn't trust women. For a long time. I walked around thinking that other women were competition or, at the very least, going to let me down in some way. Ultimately, these false beliefs, ones that were piled onto my psyche from crappy experiences at an early age, fell apart, and I came back to what I know is TRUTH: women need to be with other women. Why? Because:

Women learn by osmosis. Seriously. We absorb energy. Ever notice when you spend enough time with someone, you start to talk, move and react like they do?

Women pick up signals. No matter what kind of game face you've got on, a woman knows what's up with you. She can tell if you're BS-ing—most especially yourself.

Women gather. This one's from cave people time. It's in our DNA to collect things, share stories and create a tight knit community together.

When you take the time to surround yourself with good women, women who can support your dreams, women who are willing to see you thrive, women who know the power of being with other women—your life will be richer (in spirit and in the bank).

I regularly hear from female clients (prospective and current) that "I'm not comfortable with women." Well, the uncomfortable answer to that one is:

that's because you're not comfortable BEING a woman. What you resist persists, and does so loudly.

It's mandatory that women step up to the plate, look in the mirror and get really acquainted with themselves. Deeply intimate. Know thyself. Can this be scary? Sure. But can you really wait any longer?

TAKE THE SENSUALLY EMPOWERED WOMAN CHALLENGE THIS MONTH

- Take action in getting to know yourself, truly. Work with a coach, therapist or healer if you really want to make quantum leaps.
- Find a tribe of women who will lift you up.
- Honor the women in your life that are already a part of your tribe. Call them just to say "I'm grateful for you." Send them a handwritten card (remember those?). Take them out for a coffee or cocktail.
- Find some reverence for your mother, no matter what's gone down between you.

Engaging in the above brings you more joy, confidence and vitality.

FIND YOUR ME SPOT

MORE, MORE, MORE notes

~VILLE VALO
"Women are always beautiful."

DEBORAH KAGAN

MORE, MORE, MORE notes

~CAMILLE PAGLIA
"Women are in league with each other, a secret conspiracy of hearts and pheromones."

After Glow

*"If we are facing in the right direction,
all we have to do is keep on walking."*
~Buddhist saying

Right on! You made it. Was it as good for you as it was for me? Experiencing fifty-seven new ways to live a turned-on life is no small feat. It's something to be celebrated. So a big kudos to you, my friend.

The really fun part is that this is just the beginning of the journey. There's a whole world waiting for you. Your unique brilliance is needed. I know it might feel scary. You're on sensory megaload. Everything feels larger than life. That's a good thing. It means you're perked up. Alive. In tune. Keep going. Just like the various steps that brought you to this place, there are more to take to expand your life over and over. Because, frankly, that's what we're here to do. Expand, transform, live and love. Expand, transform, live and love. It's a guaranteed pattern for as long as we're alive and kickin'. The Find Your ME Spot tools are now forever a part of your life's tool kit, there to reference any time you're starting to feel lost and numbed out (because it will happen, no matter what stage of life you're moving through.). To help you keep moving forward in your most prosperous, abundant life, you can find additional tools and bonuses at www.deborah-kagan.com. And if you're serious about making a big leap, I offer various programs to support you in becoming your most sensually empowered self. Whether you're a lone wolf or run with the pack, I'm always here to offer guidance—and a loving kick in the butt when it's necessary. Whatever you decide to take as your next steps, drop me a line and let me know how you're doing and what's working for you. You can find me on Twitter (www.twitter.com/deborahkagan) or Facebook (www.facebook.com/mojorecoveryspecialist) where you'll also receive daily inspiration and tips for uncovering your most sensual self.

I honestly loved writing this book for you and I hope you are groovin' on your ME spot in a bigger, bolder and more luscious way than ever before. So take your fabulous self and get out there. A whole world of sensuality awaits you…and I, for one, cannot wait to see you shine!

Praise for Deborah Kagan

"After working with Deborah, I felt stronger, more creative AND my sex life got better."

~A. Goldfarb, Nutritionist

"I am writing to you to let you know that I found the love of my life!!! Yes, my soul mate!!! We are in love and I am so very happy! So thank you again and again for all your support!"

~I. Unruh, President, Kontakto

"You are the doc of all docs! I closed a deal for a raise and promotion at work. AND we found out on Valentine's Day that we are pregnant. Thank you. I know your energy, knowledge and compassion helped us to receive these gifts."

~J. Colbert, Casting Director/Producer

"Boy did our last session rock my world! Since then, my rate doubled! I am making more money now than I ever have - and really transmuting some old energy about wealth! Honestly, I just appreciate the hell out of you. I can't imagine where my life would be without the this work."

~M. Johnson, Television Producer

"Something really interesting happened to me over the last few weeks - suddenly men are asking me out all the time! I feel as if something has shifted and it's really amazing. So I just wanted to let you know that things seem to be going well and to thank you as well for your help, guidance and support."

~R. Gallaghan, Production Coordinator

"We've been thinking a lot about you lately and would like you to know how much better the IMF is doing thanks to your help. We can't believe how much better we are doing this year compared to last year. It's truly remarkable. I don't know how to thank you enough. Last year, I was so afraid that we were going to go under financially. Well, I'm thrilled to report that this year the IMF is experiencing a 77% increase over last year. And the positive attitude in the office is amazing. It's been quite a year and we'd love to set up an appointment with you for round 2!"

~S. Novis, President. IMF

"I definitely feel a shift in the energy! For a start, I have just been offered a job to work on a Broadway show opening here in Paris. I've been trying to get a job in theater and here it is! I feel as though I'm having a great life all of a sudden and am very happy. Thank you. Your consultation made such a difference to my life, to my career, to my career transition and I can't thank you enough for that."

~J. Hooker, Senior Manager

"Your responsiveness never ceases to inspire me. Thank you AGAIN for being the true catalyst to encouraging things to finally shift in my life. I am already starting to feel more free of the previous entrapments and inertia. Things are starting to flow."

~T. Murray, owner Button Bright Inc

About the Author

DEBORAH KAGAN, Sensual Lifestyle Specialist, delights in guiding women like you into living their most exciting, turned-on lives possible. For as long as she can remember, Deborah has had an innate interest in, and understanding of, the sensual nature of the world. A graduate of NYU and a native New Yorker who transplanted to Los Angeles in 1994, Deborah has taken her experiences as a prominent Feng Shui consultant, producer of V-Day Santa Monica, creator of Atma Jewels, as well as being a writer, dancer, certified yoga teacher and avid traveller, and rolled them all up into one luscious business. Her one-on-one, group and home study programs will lead you into your most juicy, fabulous self. She'd love to meet you! Visit her at www.deborah-kagan.com.

Connect with Deborah Kagan

Become a fan on Facebook:
www.facebook.com/mojorecoveryspecialist.com

Follow her on Twitter:
/deborahkagan

Find a coaching program that's right for you:
support@deborah-kagan.com

Send your comments and testimonials:
info@deborah-kagan.com

Visit her on the web at www.deborah-kagan.com

www.ingramcontent.com/pod-product-compliance
Lightning Source LLC
Chambersburg PA
CBHW070804100426
42742CB00012B/2245